PETS of the PRESIDENTS

by *Janet V. Caulkins*

The Millbrook Press
Brookfield, Connecticut

For Terence, Dan, and Sarah

Cover photograph courtesy of JFK Library
Photographs courtesy of The White House: pp. 6, 65 (David Valdez),
63 (Carol T. Powers); The Bettmann Archive: pp. 10, 16; Library of
Congress: pp. 13, 25, 28, 32, 39; Lloyd Ostendorf: pp. 18, 21;
Theodore Roosevelt Collection, Harvard College Library: p. 22;
Ohio Historical Society: p. 34; UPI/Bettmann: pp. 37, 45, 46;
JFK Library: pp. 49, 53; LBJ Library: pp. 56, 59.

Library of Congress Cataloging-in-Publication Data

Caulkins, Janet.
Pets of the presidents / by Janet V. Caulkins.
p.   cm.
Includes bibliographical references (p. 69) and index.
Summary: Relates the stories of nine American presidents and their pets,
from Thomas Jefferson's mockingbird Dick to George Bush's dog Millie.
ISBN 1-56294-060-0
1. Presidents—United States—History—Juvenile literature.
2. Pets—United States—History—Juvenile literature.
[1. Presidents—History. 2. Pets—History.] I. Title.
E176.1.C265 1992
973'.0992—dc20
[B]   91-33179   CIP   AC

Contents

Pets of the Presidents

★
---

*President George Bush takes a break from his work at the
White House to play with his spaniel Millie.*

The White House has been home to many animals, but not all were pets. Some creatures were very unwelcome—like the cockroaches that scuttled around in the kitchens from the time of Adams (1797) to the time of Truman (1945). Rats, too, have been a problem since the early days of the White House. The rats came like armies from the park across the street. At night they would scurry over and get into the White House basement. They lived among the rafters in Teddy Roosevelt's time; they stole a ham from President Lyndon Johnson; and President Bush had to fish a rat out of the swimming pool, where it had decided to take a swim with Mrs. Bush.

Other animals were brought to the White House to be useful. President Taft kept a cow (called Pauline Wayne) on the White House lawn to provide milk for the White House. President Wilson kept sheep there, and a tobacco-chewing ram named Old Ike. He kept the sheep for their wool during World War I. Calvin Coolidge kept chickens in order to eat them and save money. And before the automobile was invented, all the presidents had to have horses, just to get around.

But pets are animals we choose to keep us company, not just because they are useful. Today, in fact, some animal lovers refuse to use the word "pet." They like to speak of their "animal companions," instead.

It is true that animals have been close companions to many of our presidents. The job of the president is probably the hardest job in the nation. And the White House can be a very lonely place—partly because it is so full of people! It is the only house in the world that is the home of the nation's leader and a public museum at the same time. When you live in this public museum and you are the president, people are always coming after you to ask you for something. Pets ask only for affection.

Many presidents have found comfort and pleasure in the company of their pets. This book describes nine of our presidents. Some, like Teddy Roosevelt, have had many animals, while others like Franklin Roosevelt and George Bush have cared especially for one or two. But all the presidents in this book have had a special feeling for the companionship of animals.

THOMAS

"How he loved the bird!"

JEFFERSON

Thomas Jefferson was the first president to open the White House to the public. He thought it was important for everyone to be able to visit, even though it made him feel as if he were living in a zoo. Jefferson became president in 1801. He took the job out of a sense of duty to his country, but he didn't like it. Jefferson wrote the Declaration of Independence that made America a nation, and he was very, very proud of that. But he hated being president.

Jefferson said he could not wait to escape from the "shackles of power." Shackles are chains, and Jefferson felt chained to his job of running the country. Too often it seemed to mean holding long dreary meetings and giving enormous parties. Jefferson preferred the company of his special pet—and that was a bird, as we shall see.

Jefferson the man ★ Jefferson was long and tall. His face was sunburned and freckled, and he looked like a country farmer.

★

Jefferson was a man of many interests, from government to science.

Sometimes he answered the door himself in bedroom slippers and old corduroy knickers. That shocked many of the important people who came, all dressed up, to see him.

What really interested Jefferson was—well, everything except official meetings and being in charge of the government. He was interested in American Indians, and he often invited chiefs and their wives to official receptions. He had a collection of fossils, and he kept the skeleton of a mammoth in the big unfinished East Room of the White House, where parties and receptions are held today. Jefferson played the violin. And he liked good food. In Europe Jefferson had tasted many foods that were still unknown at home. In the White House he served ice cream, waffles, and macaroni to surprise his guests, who had never tasted such strange and wonderful things.

Jefferson had several dogs, but the surprising fact is, he did not like dogs much. He even wrote to a friend: "I would . . . join in any plan of exterminating the whole race." Jefferson thought of dogs as a real danger to sheep, which were very important to farmers in Virginia.

But one kind of dog, a French sheepdog, did interest Jefferson. These dogs were good at taking care of sheep (instead of killing and eating them). Jefferson himself went on a miserable muddy scramble through the French mountains in the rain, looking without success for a shepherd with just the right dog. Finally two dogs, Armandy and Bergère, went sent over from France just before Jefferson became president. Jefferson wanted to breed them in the United States because, he said, they were "the most careful, intelligent dogs in the world." It is too bad that today we don't even know exactly how these French sheepdogs looked.

Dick, the mockingbird ★ Birds, not dogs, were the animals that Jefferson really loved. Like Teddy Roosevelt, who was president one hundred years later, Jefferson kept records of all the birds he saw around the White House. And a mockingbird became his special pet.

Mockingbirds are known for imitating just about any sound or song. (That is why they are called mockingbirds, of course.) In those days, mockingbirds were sold in cages. A singing mockingbird cost about ten or fifteen dollars, and Jefferson bought three or four of them. Aside from imitating other birds, two of these tame birds could warble popular tunes—even French and German folk tunes. Jefferson admired mockingbirds so much that he wrote that all children should be taught great respect for these birds. He said children should be told that a mockingbird would *haunt* them if they did it any harm or stole its eggs!

One of the mockingbirds was Jefferson's favorite. He called it Dick, and he kept it in his study, where its cage hung among roses and geraniums that he grew on the windowsills. Dick spent a lot of time out of his cage, flying around the study. He would perch on Jefferson's shoulder and listen to him humming (for Jefferson used to hum to himself while he worked). Dick would watch with his head on one side while Jefferson took gardening tools out of his desk drawer to dig around in the plants in the window. When Jefferson went up to his room for a rest, the bird followed him up the stairs—hop, hop, hop, one step at a time. Upstairs, it would perch on Jefferson's couch and sing him to sleep.

Jefferson got up early in the morning by candlelight and warmed himself in front of the fireplace (for there was no other

A mockingbird can screech or squawk—or sing like an angel.
Jefferson's bird liked to sing along with Jefferson's violin.

heating in the White House). When he went down to his study, he would offer the mockingbird bits of food. Sometimes Jefferson would put a piece of fruit or bread between his lips, and raise his head. The mockingbird would flutter down and daintily take it from him. When Jefferson tucked his violin under his chin and began to play, the mockingbird would get excited and pour out his song along with the violin. It must have been a wonderful duet to hear.

A woman who knew Jefferson once wrote: "How he loved the bird! He could not live without something to love and in the absence of his darling grandchildren his bird and his flowers became the objects of his tender care."

In 1809, Jefferson finally got his wish to leave the White House and take his mockingbirds, his books and maps, and the fossils home to Monticello, the beautiful house he had built on a hilltop in Virginia.

ABRAHAM

"The kindest goats in the world"

LINCOLN

Abraham Lincoln was even taller than Jefferson. Many people found him plain, even ugly, with his long dangling arms and legs like poles. He had a large nose and bushy eyebrows. But his expression was warm and kind, and many thought it noble. When he laughed or smiled his face lit up so everyone around him felt like smiling, too. But most of the time he looked sad. An artist who knew him said that sadness "dripped from him as he walked."

Abe Lincoln was president from 1861 to 1865, during the American Civil War. The North and the South were fighting each other. It was a long, bloody war, and Washington was just "one big hospital," full of wounded and dying soldiers. The president was worried and tired all the time. Almost the only cheerful moments he had were with his children, and of course where the children were, there were the family pets.

Lincoln and his wife, Mary, had four children. One son, Edward, had died early, and one, Robert, went away to college.

*Young Tad
Lincoln was
not a very
good reader.
Lincoln tried
to help him
and read to
him often.*

But the two littlest boys, Tad and Willie, lived in the White House with their parents. Tad was seven and Willie was ten. Lincoln could sometimes be seen galloping through the halls on his storklike legs with Tad on his shoulders or laying his great length down on the floor to roll around with the boys and their kittens.

Pigs, horses, and dogs ★ Lincoln always had great tenderness for animals. As a child he'd had a little piglet that he took everywhere. When the pig grew to enormous size, as pigs will, young Lincoln rode around on him just as if he were a pony. Lincoln also had many dogs in his lifetime. There is a famous statue of him as a young man. He stands stroking the head of a dog, which leans against his leg. Probably the dog was Jip, Lincoln's favorite foxhound. The huge statue by Paul Manship is called "The Hoosier Youth." (A Hoosier was the nickname for someone who came from Indiana, where Lincoln lived from age six to age twenty.)

As a country lawyer Lincoln also had horses, which he rode from town to town. He gave them comfortable names, like Old Tom, Old Buck, and finally Old Bob, who outlived Lincoln himself. But before the Lincoln family went to the White House, they had a dog that was a favorite of all. Even Mrs. Lincoln liked him, and she had never, *never* cared for pets. The dog was a friendly yellowish sort of mutt called Fido. Happy Fido was always spoiled by Lincoln and the children. Lincoln used to feed him scraps at the dinner table, and he was even allowed to sleep on the children's beds.

When Lincoln was named to run for president, strangers paid so much attention to Fido that the poor dog spent most of

his time under the sofa, trying to get away from everyone who wanted his paw prints for souvenirs. The new president decided sadly that Fido would not be happy at the White House. The Lincolns gave Fido to some friends who had two children. But the president made his friends promise that Fido could come indoors whenever he wanted and that he would never be scolded or tied up.

In the White House ★ Nowadays in the White House, the president and his family have a lot of private space to live in. But in Lincoln's day there were only a few rooms for the family, and the rest of the house was full all day long with throngs of tourists and official callers and newspaper people. Willie and Tad refused to stay in the family rooms. Both boys had ponies that they rode around the White House grounds, and indoors the children romped all over the White House.

The president never shooed the boys away, even when he was working or meeting with government people, who used to get exasperated—especially with Tad. Tad's "black eyes fairly sparkled with mischief." He was even known to pull the beard of a dignified visitor.

Not long after the family moved into the White House, Willie got sick and could not be cured. He died in 1862, and the president was choked with grief. One day, two years after Willie's death, the stable burned, and Willie's pony was killed in the fire. The pony was especially dear to the president because it had been Willie's. He rushed out of the White House and tried to get into the burning stable to save the pony, but he was too late. The president could hardly bear it, and he was depressed for days after the fire.

Nanny and Nanko ★ After Willie's death, Lincoln kept little Tad closer than ever before and let him have anything he wanted. That was probably not good for Tad, but Lincoln couldn't help himself. That was when the goats came into the family. Tad begged for a goat (which were often pets in those days), and Lincoln bought him a pair for five dollars each. Their names were Nanny and Nanko, and they were endless trouble. Nanny, especially, liked to jump into the flower beds and munch up the blossoms. But the president refused to get rid of his pestiferous pets.

Lincoln had harnesses made, and the goats were hitched

up to a little cart. Tad and his friends would get in the cart and hold the reins while Nanny and Nanko pulled them around the grounds. Sometimes the goats went where they were told, and sometimes they pulled the cart wherever they felt like it (the flower beds again!).

Nanny was worse than Nanko when it came to destroying flower beds, so Lincoln said Tad could bring her into the house. Sometimes she even slept on Tad's bed. Soon *both* goats were allowed indoors to play.

One day Tad harnessed up the goats to a kitchen chair. Nanny and Nanko pulled Tad right through the big East Room (where Jefferson had kept his mammoth skeleton). By now the East Room was very elegant, and it was used for seeing visitors. Tad and his racing goats broke up a tea party and set the tea-cups clattering. Mrs. Lincoln was extremely cross. She did not like the goats at all, but she couldn't do anything about that, for the fact is that Lincoln loved them as much as Tad did.

Mrs. Lincoln's personal maid, Elizabeth Keckley, was amused at the president and his goats. He said to her, "Come here and look at my two goats . . . See how they sniff the clear air, and skip and play in the sunshine. Whew! What a jump! Did you ever before see such an active goat?" She tells us the goats "knew the sound of his voice, and when he called them they would come bounding to his side." Lincoln and Tad would play for hours in the yard with Nanny and Nanko, and Lincoln said they were "the kindest and best goats in the world."

Just as the Civil War was finally won by the North, Lincoln was killed. He was shot one evening at the theater by the actor John Wilkes Booth. Tad and his mother had to leave the White House, and the goats were given away. Lincoln's body and Willie's were taken back to their hometown of Springfield, Illinois. The funeral procession was followed by Lincoln's aging horse Old Bob, all draped in black. The dog Fido was still living in Springfield, but the next year Fido was assassinated, too. He came up to sniff at a man who was drunk and lying in the street. The man pulled a knife and stabbed Fido. Only Old Bob was left of the Lincoln pets, and he lived to a ripe old age in Springfield.

★

Old Robin, always known as Old Bob, in front
of Lincoln's house in Springfield, Illinois.

Teddy Roosevelt and Skip, a favorite dog,
relax on a trip out West in 1905.

THEODORE

"Lizards, guinea-pigs and ponies"

ROOSEVELT

Thousands of American children have owned and loved a teddy bear without knowing that "Teddy" was named after the 26th president of the United States, Theodore Roosevelt.

Roosevelt was usually called TR, but he was also called Teddy. Once, on a hunting trip, he refused to shoot a mother bear who had a little cub. Newspapers took up the story, and stuffed toy "Teddy Bears" sold like Ninja Turtles. The cub and the Teddy Bear became symbols of Teddy Roosevelt, one of the best-loved presidents in our history.

TR was interested in animals of all kinds, and his White House was just crammed full of pets. When he became president in 1901, TR brought his wife, Edith, and six children to the White House. From outside, the building looked quite similar to today's White House, but inside it was actually much smaller. The president, his wife, the family servants, and all the children had to be squeezed somehow into about eight upstairs rooms (including two bathrooms). It was even more crowded when you added the Roosevelt pets—more than could be counted.

TR called his children "the bunnies." The smallest was three-year-old Quentin. The president called him "Quenty-Quee." The oldest was mischievous Alice, seventeen. In between were Ted, fourteen; Kermit, twelve; Ethel, ten; and Archie, seven. And they all had animals. As a friend wrote:

> *And there were puppies, little cats,*
> *And lots of other pets and cronies,*
> *Like pink-eyed rabbits, piebald rats,*
> *And lizards, guinea-pigs and ponies.*

There were also ducks in the fountain, a badger, a pig, some snakes, a horned toad, horses, and a mean blue macaw.

Algonquin ★ Algonquin was the pony—a tiny calico Icelandic pony "like a dog, and the most absolute pet of them all," TR said. Algonquin grazed on the White House lawn and was always ready to play. Officially he was Archie's pony, but everyone, from the president down to little roly-poly Quentin, loved him and played with him. Algonquin was a frisky pony. Sometimes he would put his head down and buck when he knew his young rider was not paying attention. He bucked Ethel clean over his head one day. He also enjoyed chasing cows, but no one could stay angry with him for long.

One day, when Archie was in bed, very sick with measles, Quentin had the bright idea that a visit with Algonquin would make Archie feel better. Wicked Alice was ready to help, of course. Patting his soft nose, and whispering to him, the children smuggled the little pony into the White House elevator and took him up two floors to Archie's room for a visit.

★

Archie on Algonquin. Everyone loved the
mischievous little Icelandic pony.

★ **25** ★

No one tells what happened after that, or if Quentin and Alice were punished for this deed, but it is unlikely. Teddy Roosevelt was seldom bothered by his children's pranks. He came down hard on rudeness or cheating, but he loved to see rambunctious high spirits. TR himself liked to join in a good pillow fight at bedtime or a rainy-day game of hide-and-seek with the children in the White House attic. A pony in the house would not have disturbed him at all. In any case, Archie got well—and Algonquin did not catch the measles from Archie, in case you wondered.

Snakes galore ★ Quentin and Alice were both the owners of snakes. The real snake lover in the family seems to have been Quentin. He was just fascinated by them. The president wrote that when Quentin was around nine, he was loaned some snakes by the owner of an animal store. TR said they were "a large and beautiful and very friendly king snake and two little wee snakes."

Quentin came tearing into the White House to show these wonderful snakes to his father, who was having a meeting with an important government official. Quentin spilled the snakes right into his father's lap, where the big king snake started trying to eat the two small snakes. TR suggested that Quentin go into the next room, where four congressmen were waiting. The president said the snakes would make their waiting time more lively. What a scene!

Alice Roosevelt's snake was different; it was "a little cool green snake." She called it Emily Spinach—Emily "in honor of a very thin aunt, and spinach because it was green." In truth, Alice especially enjoyed making people jump and gasp by showing off the harmless little snake in company.

The rest of the zoo ★ Alice had another troublesome pet—a large blue macaw that little Quentin called a "polly parrot." This scary bird with its great sharp beak was named Eli Yale. Eli lived in a room filled with ferns, palms, and other plants. He ate a starchy diet of bread and potatoes, and for some strange reason he also liked coffee grounds.

Eli had the plant room pretty much to himself because he liked to bite. The big blue bird was fond of Ted, TR's oldest son. But the maids and everyone else, including the president, were all scared to death of him. TR said Eli was a bird with "a bill that I think could bite through boiler plate, who crawls all over Ted and whom I view with dark suspicion."

Eli the macaw may have been just about the only animal that TR "viewed with suspicion." The White House was full to the rafters with furry, crawling, slithering, bouncing, flying, or scampering pets. There was a very small, unusually good tempered badger named Josiah, or Josh for short. TR had found him on an expedition in the Grand Canyon and fed him on milk and potatoes (sort of like the macaw).

What else could there be? Well, there was a piebald rat "of a most affectionate nature," the president said, and a jumping kangaroo rat, and whole families of guinea pigs. Little Ethel allowed the president to baby-sit her guinea pigs. The president wrote, "At this moment I am acting as nurse to two wee guinea pigs which Ethel feels would not be safe, save in the room with me."

Cats, dogs, and horses ★ Of course there were horses, cats, and dogs at the Roosevelt White House. Teddy Roosevelt was a wonderful horseman. In 1898, before he became president, there was a war between Spain and the United States. TR organized

Ted with the fearsome blue macaw. TR said the bird's bill could bite through metal plate.

a volunteer cavalry that became famous during the war as the Rough Riders. And the president had once owned a ranch out West, where he rode every day. One of his aides claimed that TR was "one of the best riders in the world." At the White House, the Roosevelts had many horses. TR's favorite horse was Bleistein, who was a great jumper.

Cats and dogs came and went during the eight years the Roosevelts were in the White House. There were two favorite cats: Slippers and Tom Quartz. Tom Quartz was a kitten named after a character in *Roughing It,* by Mark Twain. Tom Quartz made a game of jumping out at people and wrapping his little paws around their legs. When there was no person to play with, he would pounce on one of the dogs, who put up with him patiently.

Slippers was a soft gray cat. He was called Slippers because he had extra toes, which gave him big paddy feet. He liked to take walks with the Roosevelts and their little dog Skip. Slippers padded along in his six-toed way with a loudly tinkling bell around his neck to warn the birds away. Like Thomas Jefferson, TR loved birds, and he knew a lot about them. He knew dozens of bird calls, and he kept lists of the birds that came and went around the White House grounds.

Skip: "A happy little life" ★ The Roosevelts had many dogs, and if one died or was lost, another one would soon join the family. Little Skip was a favorite of the president's. He was a terrier that TR had picked up during one of his trips in the Grand Canyon. TR said Skip was a good hunter and fighter and would stand his ground before a bear or a lynx at bay. But Skip was also a loving little dog. He would get tired on the long trail, and he liked to ride cuddled in front of the president on his saddle. Skip was TR's dog, but after the president brought him back to the White House, Skip often jumped into Archie's bed and snuggled up for company at night.

Skip also became a close friend of Archie's pony, Algonquin. When Algonquin saw Skip coming, he would pretend to run away. But he would watch from the corner of his eye and slow down a bit for Skip to catch up. Skip would come tearing alongside and jump up on Algonquin's back for a ride.

Skip loved games, and Archie used to have races with him in the wide second-floor hall of the White House. TR wrote: Archie "spreads his legs, bends over and holds Skip between them. Then he says, 'On your mark, Skip, ready!; go!' and shoves Skip back while he runs as hard as he possibly can to the other end of the hall, Skip scrambling wildly with his paws on the smooth floor . . ."

When the children were not at home, Skip was lonely. Then he would go and find the president, and TR would let him hop up for a snooze in his lap while he was reading. Skip died in 1907 when Archie was thirteen. He had "a happy little life," said TR.

TR and conservation ★ Teddy Roosevelt, we know, loved nature and animals, and he passed this love on to his children. But more important, he saw to it that great areas of wilderness and wildlife were preserved for the American people. He used all his powers as president to help save such places as Yellowstone, the Grand Canyon, and Yosemite. Of all the presidents who loved animals and nature, Teddy Roosevelt must be at the top of the list.

WARREN G.

Laddie Boy, the important Airedale

HARDING

Warren Harding was president from 1921 to 1923. He was handsome, and he looked most dignified. But he chewed tobacco in private and used a toothpick at the White House dinner table. He was the first president to hire someone else to write his speeches for him.

Harding had a dog that was famous all over the land. He was a big pedigreed Airedale named Caswell Laddie Boy. He wore dog license No. 1 and went to official meetings. He sat right up at the table among the president's advisers, just like one of them. Only a few White House dogs have been so well known to the public. A Scottie called Fala, two beagles named Him and Her, and a springer spaniel called Millie also became famous and popular, as we shall see.

The president and his wife, Florence, were true animal lovers. Mrs. Harding had birdhouses set up around the White House grounds. They were specially designed to attract the many different species of birds around Washington. When the pres-

President Harding wanted Laddie Boy to be in his photograph.
Laddie Boy wanted to take the president for a walk instead.

ident discovered that a pair of owls had hatched three chicks in a tree near the White House, he was very excited. As long as the baby owls stayed in the nest, the president would often go and visit the tree to check up on them.

The Hardings had several dogs besides Laddie Boy, but Laddie Boy was the animal that really meant the most to President Harding. Laddie Boy saw the president through some very hard times. A woman who knew Laddie Boy well said, "He helped the Hardings over the rough spots."

President Harding was very popular when he first came to the White House in 1921. He promised the nation that everything would stay peaceful and "normal" while he was president. But Harding had some dishonest friends, and he was a man who could never say "no" to his friends. Before long the president and others were accused of dishonest business deals. The president was very unhappy. He said, "I have no trouble with my enemies . . . but my friends . . . they're the ones who keep me walking the floor nights!" Laddie Boy was a great comfort to him. The president knew that his dog was one friend who would not let him down.

Laddie Boy knew the president by his first name. Mrs. Harding would give Laddie Boy the newspaper and say, "Take it to Warren," and Laddie Boy would trot off to find the president and deliver the paper.

Laddie Boy was helpful in other ways, too: Sometimes the Hardings would have a fight and refuse to speak to each other until the bad temper wore off. Instead, they would talk to each other by pretending to talk to Laddie Boy. They would tell him whatever they wanted the other person to hear. Laddie Boy could never figure out what was going on. He thought they were really talking to him.

★

---

*Laddie Boy, enthroned in his important chair. He seems to
be waiting for reporters to come and interview him.*

Laddie Boy was almost always with the president. For official meetings he had his own carved, high-backed chair. He was well known to reporters. There were pretend interviews with Laddie Boy on every kind of topic, from votes for women to animal rights to the theories of the scientist Albert Einstein.

The president treated Laddie Boy just like a person. The big dog even had his own personal servant, whose name was Willie Jackson. On Laddie Boy's birthday there was a doggy party with a birthday cake made out of many layers of dog biscuits covered with white icing. It is not reported if the icing was made of sugar—maybe it was bacon fat.

President Harding died suddenly in 1923 when he was returning from a trip to Alaska. Rumors flew about that Laddie Boy had a feeling that something would happen to his master, and that he howled for three days before the president's death. In any case, he was a very sad dog. He kept waiting for his master to come home. Everytime he heard the sound of a car arriving he perked up his ears, but the president never came.

After President Harding died, Laddie Boy was given away, but a statue of him was made as a present for Mrs. Harding. It is said that the statue was paid for by the newsboys of America, because President Harding had once been a newsboy himself. Newsboys across the country were asked to give one penny each to pay for the statue.

CALVIN

A raccoon named Rebecca

COOLIDGE

Some people thought that President Calvin Coolidge liked animals better than human beings. Coolidge was president from 1923 to 1929. He was a small man with a smooth face and round glasses. He didn't smile much. He would look at people through his round glasses and then turn away. He didn't like conversation. He talked so little he was known as Silent Cal, and people found him very hard to know. But Coolidge liked animals very much, and he had lots of cats and dogs.

Silent Cal liked the company of his pets much better than a roomful of chattering guests. He used to feed his cats himself in the dining room. There is a story that once when the president had an important guest, he poured some cream into a saucer at the table without a word of explanation. After a minute, the confused guest decided he should do that, too, just to be polite. Then Coolidge just smiled and put his saucer on the floor for the cat. The story may be true because Silent Cal liked to play little jokes on people. He would press all the buttons

★

President Coolidge, just back from a fishing trip, shows the trout he caught to Mrs. Coolidge, Rob Roy, and Prudence Prim.

that called different White House servants and aides. He thought it was funny to hear all the doors banging open and see people running from all over to see what the president wanted.

Mrs. Coolidge's name was Grace, and she was the opposite of Silent Cal. She loved to laugh and have fun. She, too, liked animals, especially dogs and birds. The Coolidges had an Airedale named Paul Pry and two white collies named Prudence Prim and Rob Roy. Grace Coolidge had lots of fun with the dogs. One Easter she dressed them in Easter bonnets for the Easter egg roll on the White House lawn. Prudence Prim even wore a black veil. It may seem silly to dress up dogs like people, but the dogs didn't seem to mind.

Lillian Parks, the daughter of the White House head maid, wrote about the Coolidge dogs. She thought the Coolidges and their dogs were funny. She wrote that "Mrs. Coolidge had only to whistle and the dogs would come bounding to her, but the President had to whistle until he was blue in the face to get their attention." The president finally got a little whistle that he "blew like a locomotive" when he wanted to call the dogs.

Rob Roy ★ The white collie Rob Roy posed with Mrs. Coolidge for her portrait. You can see the painting today if you visit the White House. She is standing in a long red dress, with the white collie by her side. (President Coolidge wanted her to wear a white dress, and suggested that they could dye the dog red for contrast!) Mrs. Coolidge got the rambunctious Rob Roy to sit still by feeding him candy during the sitting. It probably was very bad for Rob Roy, but people didn't know as much then about healthy diets as we do today—so Rob Roy got all the candy he wanted.

Mrs. Coolidge and Prudence Prim in their best bonnets.

There were lots of other dogs in the Coolidge household, including several chows, a bulldog, a Shetland sheepdog, a German shepherd, and a terrier. Lillian Parks remembers that Rob Roy was boss of them all: "He showed them what to do and taught them how to keep the maids around the White House in a state of terror. The dogs would run through the halls after him like a burst of bullets, and all the maids would run for cover."

Parks goes on to say, "Rob Roy was a perfect angel with the first family. When the President took his nap, Rob Roy would stretch out on the window seat near him like a perfect gentleman. . . . He would not make a sound until the President had wakened and left for the office; then he would bark to let everyone know the coast was clear." She adds that Rob Roy's bark was a signal for the other dogs to come running, and a sign for all the maids to watch out!

Birds and cats ★ President and Mrs. Coolidge also had many birds. "There was one huge myna bird," writes Lillian Parks, "which would alight on everyone's shoulder and pinch their ears. Mama had a terrible time with the myna, because he would ride around on top of her head when she was tidying the room, and if she pushed him off, he would resent it." She doesn't say what the myna bird did when it resented you. Maybe it liked to pull people's hair.

Aside from Rob Roy, the white collie, President Coolidge liked cats best. Two favorites were Blackie and Tiger—they were the ones the president used to feed in the dining room. The cats were allowed to explore the whole White House. Blackie's favorite game was to ride up and down in the elevator. He would wait by the elevator doors until some kind person opened the door. Blackie would get in and stretch out on the cushioned elevator seat and just ride up and down.

Tiger didn't care about the elevator, but he liked to roam. One day he went out for a stroll and didn't come back. The president was very upset. He sent a message out over the Washington radio stations, describing Tiger. It worked, and Tiger was found. The president decided to have each cat wear a little collar with the words "the White House," so people would know where the cats belonged. One day Tiger strayed again and never did return. Maybe someone wanted to keep a cat that had belonged to the president of the United States, but President Coolidge was very sorry to lose his cat.

Rebecca ★ There was one other animal that President Coolidge kept. It was Rebecca—a raccoon. Rebecca had a special little house that was built for her outdoors. The president would go out there to play with her, and sometimes he took walks with Rebecca on a leash. Rebecca was allowed indoors at the White House, too. Every once in a while visitors would see her waddling along the halls. The visitors would think a wild animal had sneaked in. They would call the staff in great excitement, only to be told that Rebecca was just one of the family.

At the end of his first term as president, Coolidge said he would not seek a second term. But secretly he thought people would ask him to try for another term anyway. His friends kept saying, "Don't you want to run for president again?" and he kept saying "no," but meaning "yes." He was surprised and very disappointed when they believed him and he was not asked to run again. Herbert Hoover was nominated instead, and he won the election. So Rob Roy and Rebecca and the myna and the cats left the White House to make way for a new president.

FRANKLIN D.

"Fala never forgot"

ROOSEVELT

Franklin Delano Roosevelt was usually called FDR. He was a cousin of Teddy Roosevelt, who had been president fourteen years before. He was paralyzed from polio, a disease that can now be prevented. From the waist down he could hardly move. He didn't let that stop him, though. He found that he could live his life and lead his country from a wheelchair.

Roosevelt became president in 1933. He was the only president to stay in the White House for four terms in a row—almost sixteen years. When he became president, the country was suffering. There was no work. People were losing their jobs, their money, and their homes. And at the end of Roosevelt's third term the United States entered World War II. There were sad times and plenty of problems for this 32nd president of the United States.

In the midst of it all, Roosevelt was given a frisky little bright-eyed black dog—a Scottie named Fala. This intelligent furry fellow was Roosevelt's special companion and comfort to the day the president died.

Too many dogs ★ The president's family had always loved horses and dogs. After his illness, of course, FDR could never ride horseback again. But he had many dogs, and he brought them all along to the White House. FDR and his wife, Eleanor, came to the White House with five noisy, happy children and a "snowstorm of dogs"—a Great Dane, an Irish setter, a cocker spaniel, a couple of bullmastiffs, a German shepherd, and a sheepdog. The dogs all found it very hard to adjust to life in the White House. Strangers were always coming and going, cameras kept flashing, and crowds of people hurried to the huge official dinners and tea parties.

The different dogs were "all over the place," said the housekeeper, and so were the dogs of friends and assistants. The dogs chewed on the furniture and messed on the White House rugs; their scratchy toenails could be heard racing over the polished floors. Mrs. Roosevelt's Scottie Meg bit a friendly reporter on the nose. A maid describes how "the maids all had to carry feather dusters to ward off a horsey-looking Great Dane and Major, a German shepherd. . . . It was worth your life to make a bed if Major or the Great Dane were around."

Many of this crowd of rowdy dogs finally had to be sent back home to the president's house at Hyde Park, in New York. But in 1940 one small, cheerful dog pranced into the White House to become the president's own special friend, and that was Fala. As Mrs. Roosevelt said, "No dog was completely happy at the White House until Fala came."

The Outlaw of Fala Hill ★ Fala's full name was Murray the Outlaw of Fala Hill. He came to the White House just at the time World War II was beginning, and he stayed until the president died in 1945.

Fala enjoyed showing off the tricks he could do: "playing dead," sitting up, rolling over. But he was a dignified little Scottie, and he paid no attention to all the other bad-mannered White House dogs. The only time Fala's dignity was hurt was when a female Scottie, who was chosen to have Fala's puppies, bit him hard on the bottom. Fala had to go to an army hospital to get patched up.

The Boss, as FDR's family called the president, kept Fala at his side. From the start they were a team. It made people feel good just to see them together. As Lillian Parks, daughter of the White House head maid, wrote, "His heart was true, and he made it clear that he had only one master."

Fala always slept in the president's room. Sometimes the "poor little fellow" would spot the bedroom rug before he had a chance to go out. But he wanted to stay overnight with the president, and the president wanted him there. The White House beds all had silk bedspreads, but not the president's bed. He had a cotton cover so Fala and all the children could climb up while FDR had his breakfast in bed—and of course the breakfast tray always had a dog biscuit for Fala.

Wartime ★ The United States entered World War II when Japan attacked Pearl Harbor on December 7, 1941. Blackout curtains were put up in the White House so no light would show to guide enemy airplanes at night. Everyone in Washington went around with dim little flashlights. Everyone in the nation worked hard to help the war effort. Children saved paper and tin cans. Fala became an honorary private in the Army. He was pictured giving a dollar to help the war effort; and so thousands of people sent in a dollar, and their dogs became privates, too.

Fala "donated" his rubber toys in a scrap drive during
World War II. Rubber was collected, recycled, and used
to make tires and other supplies for the war effort.

Riding next to FDR with the top down was Fala's favorite sport.

Fala always traveled in the car with the president. Through the car windows his black ears could be seen sticking up beside the Boss. Reporters loved to take his picture sitting there beside FDR, looking very important. People everywhere knew him. In fact, they knew Fala so well that during the war he was nicknamed "the informer" by the men who guarded the president. The president's travel plans were kept secret during the war, but Fala traveled with him as usual. The Scottie insisted on being walked at every train stop, and people would see him and know that FDR must be aboard.

World War II was a terrible, long war, started by one of the most evil men the world has known—Adolf Hitler. Just as victory was in sight for the United States and its allies, President Roosevelt died. The country was shocked, and for Fala it was a mystery. He felt the way Laddie Boy had felt when Harding died. Fala just couldn't understand where his master had gone. Every time he heard a car in the driveway he would prick up his ears and get up and wave his tail, expecting to see FDR come in the door.

Fala rode in Mrs. Roosevelt's car for the president's funeral, and Mrs. Roosevelt took Fala to live with her when she left the White House, but she said he never got used to the fact that FDR was gone for good. Mrs. Roosevelt wrote: "Many dogs eventually forget. Fala never really forgot. Whenever he heard the sirens he became alert and felt again that he was an important being, as he had felt when he was traveling with Franklin."

FDR was buried in the garden at Hyde Park, and later, when he too died, so was Fala.

JOHN F.

"Be nice to those dogs!"

KENNEDY

John F. Kennedy—JFK—became president in 1960. He was the kind of person that children and dogs like right away. He had a lot of energy and a happy smile. His thick hair stood up over his forehead and made him look like a boy. He loved to joke and make up games to play with his children, three-year-old Caroline and baby John, and their pets.

Kennedy liked his children to have pets to love and care for. "Be nice to those dogs," he would say to little John, "They are your friends!" The Kennedys had almost as many pets as Theodore Roosevelt. Caroline and John kept adding to the family collection of ducks, rabbits, hamsters, guinea pigs, canaries, lovebirds, dogs, and ponies.

It was not an easy time to be president. The United States and the Soviet Union were on very unfriendly terms. It was a time known as the Cold War. There was no shooting, but the whole world was afraid the Cold War might turn into a real war at any time.

The Kennedys with just a few of the family pets.

When things got very tense, President Kennedy would sometimes call for Caroline's Welsh terrier Charlie. Just having the happy-go-lucky Charlie around was a relief from strain. The president's office door opened onto the grassy lawn, and the president would often cheer himself up by going outside and clapping his hands to call the dogs and children playing there. When they heard the clapping, the shouting children and the crowd of barking dogs would come scampering to see him. The White House dog keeper, Traphes Bryant, called this the president's "dog-and-kid routine."

Kennedy dogs ★ It is hard to believe, but John Kennedy was allergic to animal fur. It made him cough and sneeze and made his eyes itch. But that didn't stop him from keeping a whole houseful of dogs. Whenever the president came back from a trip, several of the dogs would be there to greet his helicopter as it landed. Kennedy loved being greeted by his doggy friends. It started a tradition that presidents have followed ever since.

The dog Charlie, who cheered up the president in times of crisis, also went swimming with him in the White House pool. The pool was usually full of bobbing balls and toys that the president would throw for Charlie. (There was probably quite a lot of dog hair in there, too.)

There were lots of dogs besides Charlie in the Kennedy household. There was an enormous Irish wolfhound, taller than the children. He was named Wolf. (He was nice to people, but he hated other dogs, it seems.) There was a German shepherd called Clipper. And there was another favorite, Shannon. Shannon was a fluffy Irish cocker spaniel, given to the Kennedys by the prime minister of Ireland. (Kennedy's great-grandparents had come from Ireland.)

Of all the dogs, though, Charlie was boss dog. He knew he was number one. Clipper and Wolf were much bigger than Charlie, but Charlie always put them in their place. The president thought it was funny that Charlie would growl loudly if any other dog even tried to go through a doorway before him.

But Charlie was not serious and dignified like FDR's dog Fala. Charlie was a harum-scarum pup. He chased the ducks that lived on the south lawn around the fountain. He would splash right into the fountain, sending ducks squawking in every direction. In the end, the ducks were given away because they greedily nibbled up all the young tulips in the spring.

With no ducks to annoy, Charlie got his fun by sneaking up behind White House workers and gardeners. If he saw anyone bending over, he would creep, creep, creep up quietly from the rear, and then he would bite that person on the bottom and tear off at top speed. Charlie also thought it was funny to lift his leg and wet on people who were standing around talking. Maybe it was his way of getting more attention; if so, it probably worked!

Charlie and Pushinka ★ Another important Kennedy dog was Pushinka. She was a fluffy little white mutt, and she came from the Soviet Union. Pushinka was the daughter of Strelka, one of the Soviet space dogs. Dogs were the first living things to travel in space. The Soviet Union sent several dogs up in rockets before it was safe to send humans. Strelka, Pushinka's mother, was shot into space in August 1960. Pushinka was given to the Kennedys by Premier Nikita Khrushchev of the Soviet Union, and that caused all kinds of problems. The Soviet Union was an "unfriendly nation" at the time. What did this gift mean? Was Pushinka a spy dog? The Secret Service checked Pushinka out for hidden microphones or implanted "bugs." But she was innocent, so she happily joined the Kennedy family.

Charlie took one look at this charming foreigner and fell in love. Then Charlie and Pushinka had puppies—even though Pushinka turned out to be a jealous type. Mr. Bryant, the dog keeper, reported that Charlie was jealous of Wolf, and Clipper was jealous of Shannon, but Pushinka was jealous of *everybody,* including her own four puppies. Pushinka's and Charlie's puppies were Blackie, Streaker, Butterfly, and White Tip. By this time, the Soviet Union had sent the very first Earth satellite into space. It was called Sputnik, so JFK grinned and called Pushinka's puppies "pupniks."

When they were old enough, the puppies were given away. Two were prizes in a letter-writing contest for children. Thousands of children wrote on the subject of the home and care they thought the pups should have. Since Kennedy was a Democrat, not a Republican, one boy wrote: "I will raise the dog to be a Democrat and to bite all Republicans." (He forgot to give his address, or he might have had one of the puppies.)

Ponies, birds, and hamsters ★ Of course dogs were not the only Kennedy pets. The president's wife, Jacqueline, put the children on horses before they could even walk. Baby John often rode on the saddle in front of his mother on a beautiful bay horse called Sardar, but his reaction the first time he was put on a pony alone was "I want to get off." John's pony was named Leprechaun, which is a kind of Irish elf. Caroline's pony was Macaroni.

Macaroni used to wander around on the lawn of the White House. He was very sociable—like Teddy Roosevelt's Algon-

JFK with Caroline, who rides Macaroni. Caroline won a blue ribbon on Macaroni when she was only five.

quin—and he liked people. Once the president looked up from his desk to see Macaroni peeking in the window. The president laughed and opened the door for him, but Macaroni shyly decided not to go into the office after all. He was not as bold as Algonquin, who rode in the White House elevator.

There was also a family of hamsters among the Kennedy animals. Debbie and Billie were two of them. The hamsters kept catching colds or getting lost. They were always getting into dreadful trouble. The newspapers loved stories about the hamsters. A reporter once woke up the president's assistant, Pierre Salinger, at 3 o'clock in the morning asking him to check out a report that one of the little creatures was dead. Sure enough, a hamster had slipped into the president's bathtub and drowned. (As far as we know, the president was not in the tub at the time.)

Debbie and Billie hamster had a dramatic home life. First they had babies, but Billie turned around and ate them up. Mr. Bryant, the dog keeper, adds that Debbie killed Billie in revenge "and then died herself, probably of indigestion."

John Kennedy was president for only three short years. In 1963 he was riding in an open car in Dallas, Texas. A sniper aimed a rifle through the window of a building and shot the president. The whole nation was shocked and saddened. People all over the world sent messages of sympathy. But the government had to go on. The vice president, Lyndon Johnson, became president. Mrs. Kennedy and the children moved to New York City, and almost all the pets had to be given away.

The new president, Lyndon Johnson, also loved animals, and once more a new set of White House pets moved in.

LYNDON B.

Him, Her, and Yuki

JOHNSON

Lyndon Baines Johnson, or LBJ, was a tall Texan. He was boiling with energy. He made everyone around him work hard, and he worked hard himself. Johnson loved animals, especially dogs. He took great comfort from his pets during his last years as president, when the country seemed to turn against him. People were angry because Johnson kept the United States at war in Vietnam—a war that many citizens did not support.

When Johnson was president, the White House was always full of dogs and puppies, and the president would call for them at all hours. Everyone told him not to let puppies loose on the White House rugs. The president would do it anyway, and of course the puppies always made big puddles and messes. But LBJ didn't care. He just loved "a basket full of fresh wiggly puppies" with names like Freckles and Kim and Little Chap and Dumpling and Crasher.

LBJ says hello to his favorite beagles, Him and Her. The president treated the dogs like important people, and his pockets were always filled with treats for them.

Him and Her ★ The president's favorite dogs were two beagles—small dogs with long ears. They were just called Him and Her. The beagles were treated like important people, right from the start. LBJ took them for car rides and boat rides. They traveled with him in his limousine, and if people didn't want to ride with a beagle—well, they could just go in another car. The beagle stayed with the president.

Reporters loved to write about Him and Her. The president's assistants often complained that the dogs got more publicity than the president. LBJ teased the beagle Him about that. "You'd better not try to steal the show," the president said to his dog, "or I'll ship you back to Texas!" But he never did, even when Him wet on a chair at a tea for a visiting princess.

Once, when he was showing the dogs to reporters, the president got into real trouble. He wanted to get Him and Her to stand up and bark for the reporters. So he pulled up on their long floppy ears. That hurt, and the beagles yelped. The story was in all the newspapers, and the president got angry letters from dog lovers all over the country. But LBJ didn't think ear pulling really hurt the dogs—which just shows that presidents make mistakes like everyone else.

The president really loved his dogs. His pockets were always full of dog treats, and his suits were always covered with dog hairs. The White House dog keeper said, "LBJ was the greatest pet lover I have ever known."

People must have finally forgiven the president for pulling his beagles' ears. When one of the beagles died, they sent hundreds of sympathy letters. Her had picked up a stone to play with and swallowed it by accident, and the vets could not save her. After that, the president stayed even closer to the other beagle, Him.

Blanco ★ Another important dog at the White House was Blanco, a white collie. Blanco was very nervous and jealous. He got excited one day when dog treats were being handed out, and he nipped and tore the coat of Traphes Bryant, the dog keeper. To tease the president, Mr. Bryant kept on wearing the torn coat. The president teased back. He would holler, "Mr. Bryant, why is your sleeve torn? Why are you keeping my dogs fat? Why are buttons missing from your coat?"

Yuki ★ One day, little Him was hit by a car and killed. The president was very sad. Now both his beagles were gone. Friends thought he would never again care so much about a dog. But then, on Thanksgiving Day, LBJ's daughter Luci picked up a tiny stray mutt that was whimpering in the road near the Johnson ranch in Texas. She named it Yuki and brought it to the White House. The president said Yuki was "pretty as a polecat," which was supposed to be a great compliment. He had found a new dog to love.

Yuki was white and silky, and he shed white hairs on everyone. People said the president often looked as if he were sprinkled with flour after he played with Yuki. They said he looked like a baking powder biscuit. People who didn't want to be covered with white hairs tried not to ride with the president in his limousine. The president himself complained about Yuki's shedding all the time, but he went right on playing with Yuki.

LBJ loved to joke. Just for fun, he taught Yuki to "sing." The president would throw back his head, and Yuki would throw back *his* head and start to howl, and they would howl a duet. LBJ and Yuki would get on the telephone, and they would howl their song to Mrs. Johnson when she was in Texas.

LBJ and Yuki tune up to sing a duet.

The president took Yuki everywhere. He even danced a few rounds with Yuki at his daughter Lynda's wedding. He went to the Christmas tree lighting ceremony with Yuki dressed in a red Santa Claus suit and a white beard. Once the president took Yuki into the White House bowling alley. Yuki chased a ball and almost got caught in the machinery that set up the bowling pins. Mrs. Johnson shouted to cut off the electricity, and Yuki was saved.

LBJ left the White House for good in 1969, and Yuki went with him. The president had had great ideals. "I wanted to be the president who educated young children, helped feed the hungry, helped the poor to find their way," he said. But the people could not forgive him for letting the war in Vietnam drag on. Later, he said sadly that the war had been a terrible mistake. He had lost his dream of a "Great Society." He and Mrs. Johnson went back to their ranch in Texas, and most of the dogs and puppies went to different homes. But Yuki stayed with the president and was with him when he died of a heart attack in 1973.

GEORGE

Millie and son

BUSH

When George Bush became president in 1989, he had a hard job to do and many decisions to make. America had huge debts and not enough money to help pay for such things as schools and health care. In 1990 he had to decide whether the United States should send soldiers to fight a war in the Persian Gulf. The job of president seemed harder than ever. But President Bush somehow found time for his family, including five grown children, ten grandchildren, and Millie, the Bushes' famous springer spaniel.

Millie came bouncing into the Bushes' lives shortly before George Bush became president. Her head was mostly dark, with a white streak running up between her eyes. Her muzzle was white with dark freckles, her nose was large and pink, and she had soulful golden eyes and long silky ears. Barbara Bush loved Millie from the moment she saw her, but she did think that Millie was funny looking. She whispered to the little spaniel, "You are *so* sweet, but you are *so* ugly. You have a pig's nose, you are bowlegged, and your eyes are yellow." But Millie was so happy and loving that Barbara Bush came to think Millie was the best dog the Bushes had ever had.

Millie was named Mildred Kerr Bush, after a friend from Texas. Millie had a sweet hopeful expression, and people liked to meet her. In fact Millie was photographed hundreds of times with famous people—astronauts, kings and queens, opera singers, and tennis champs. The only time Millie ever barked at a stranger was when she was introduced to the "Easter bunny." It was a man dressed up in a bunny suit. Millie was horrified to see this huge man-size rabbit, and she set up a terrible howl.

One reason Millie became so famous is that Barbara Bush wrote a book about her. In the book, Millie is the main character and tells all about her life in the White House with "George" and "Bar."

But Millie became famous also just because she was the president's dog; wherever he was, she always seemed to be around, carrying her orange tennis ball and keeping him company. When Washington newspaper writers learned that Millie was going to have puppies, they kept a "puppy watch."

Five girls and a boy ★ To get ready for the puppies, Barbara Bush prepared a "birthing room." There was a small room on the second floor of the White House that had been used as a beauty parlor. Now a big "nesting box" took the place of the hair dryers. In the box there was a special pillow made of needlepoint embroidery that Millie liked to rest her chin on. Mrs. Bush had her desk moved into the birthing room, so she could work and still keep Millie company and watch over her.

Finally the puppies were ready to be born. There was a

★

Millie in her "nesting box," waiting for her puppies to
arrive. Her head rests on her favorite needlepoint pillow.

White House dinner going on. The president couldn't leave, so after dinner Barbara Bush left the party and went upstairs to stay with Millie. The first puppy came at 9 P.M.; fifteen minutes later there was another, and then another. Millie had six puppies in all. There were five females. The sixth was a male puppy who was named Ranger.

President Bush played with the furry babies every day. He must have agreed with Lyndon Johnson, who just loved a basketful of wiggly puppies. For exercise, the six squirming little dogs were loaded into a big red plastic toy bag covered with Mickey Mouse designs. Then the whole bagful was carried downstairs and spilled out onto the grass. The president couldn't resist them. He sat on the floor or on the grass to play with the pups—even dressed in his business suit. He would just lie down on the grass and let the puppies scramble all over him.

The girl puppies were given to friends and grandchildren. As Barbara Bush said, "It is nice for children to have something warm and furry to hug." In the end, Ranger was kept by George and Barbara Bush, so Millie had company when George and Bar were busy.

Millie and Ranger at home ★ Like Millie, Ranger was allowed to sleep in the bedroom with George and Barbara Bush. At first, Millie would wake up early, and she often decided it would be a good idea to wake up the president as well. She would climb up on the bed between the president and Mrs. Bush and shake her floppy ears in their faces. That woke them up, all right!

The president and Mrs. Bush liked to read the newspapers and have coffee in bed. If the grandchildren were visiting, the bed might have coffee, juice, newspapers, Millie, Ranger, and

Millie and Ranger with President Bush in the
Oval Office. They seem to be asking the president
to take a break and play with them.

small children all bouncing around there at once. But if the president sneezed, Ranger would shoot out of there like a bullet. Maybe he was afraid of catching cold.

Around 7 o'clock, Millie and Ranger would trot along beside the president to the Oval Office, where the president works. Millie usually carried her orange tennis ball, just in case the president would take a break and go out to play with her. Ranger carried a ball, too. In fact, he would leave balls all over the place for people to trip on. Ranger just seemed to think it important to have a ball handy at all times.

Outdoors, Millie became a great squirrel hunter, tearing after the squirrels with her ears streaming out behind her. Millie's squirrel hunting really worried former president Ronald Reagan, when he heard about it. Mr. Reagan was president before George Bush, and he liked to feed the squirrels. So President Bush put up a little sign warning the squirrels about Millie. It is too bad that squirrels can't read, because Millie sometimes caught one!

Besides chasing squirrels, Millie liked to play in the flower beds. Just like President Lincoln's goat Nanny, Millie could ruin a flower bed in no time. But best of all Millie and Ranger liked playing with the president and chasing the tennis balls he hit for them—especially when the balls went into the flower beds! Then, when the dogs were good and dirty, the president or Mrs. Bush would get into the shower with them and shampoo them with dog shampoo.

George Bush, it seems, is a "two-dog man." He did not bring a lot of other pets to the White House. But Millie and Ranger seemed happy to have George and Bar all to themselves.

Notes

Jefferson: "I would join in any plan . . ." Stanton, 1989; "the most careful . . ." ibid.; "How he loved the bird . . ." from *First Forty Years of Washington Society* by Mrs. Samuel Harrison Smith, quoted in many sources, including Commager and Dos Passos.

Lincoln: sadness "dripped from him . . ." F. B. Carpenter; "black eyes fairly sparkled . . ." Keckley; "Come here and look . . . knew the sound of his voice . . . kindest and best goats in the world . . ." ibid.

Roosevelt, Theodore: "And there were puppies . . ." Poem by poet Arthur Guterman, quoted in Hagedorn; "Like a dog . . ." *Theodore Roosevelt's Letters to His Children;* "a large and beautiful king snake . . ." ibid.; "a little cool green snake . . ." Longworth; "a bill that could bite . . ." *Theodore Roosevelt's Letters;* "At this moment . . ." ibid.; "one of the best riders . . ." Depew; "spreads his legs . . ." *Theodore Roosevelt's Letters;* "a happy little life . . ." ibid.

Harding: "he helped the Hardings . . ." quoted in Bryant; "I have no trouble . . ." quoted in Seale, vol. 2.

Coolidge: "Mrs. Coolidge had only to whistle . . ." Parks; "blew like a loco-motive" Hoover; "He showed them what to do . . ." ibid.; "Rob Roy was a perfect angel . . ." ibid.; "There was one huge myna bird . . ." ibid.

Roosevelt, Franklin D.: "snowstorm of dogs" Parks; "the maids all had to carry feather dusters . . ." ibid.; "No dog was completely happy . . ." Eleanor Roosevelt, *This I Remember;* "His heart was true . . ." Parks; "poor little fellow . . ." Nesbitt; "the informer" Seuling; "Many dogs forget . . ." Eleanor Roosevelt, *On My Own.*

Kennedy: "Be nice to those dogs . . ." Bryant; "dog-and-kid routine . . ." ibid.; "I will raise the dog . . ." Salinger; "I want to get off" quoted in Truman; "and then died . . ." Bryant.

Johnson: "a basket full of fresh wiggly puppies" Bryant; "You'd better not try . . ." ibid.; "LBJ was the greatest . . ." ibid.; "Mr. Bryant, why is your sleeve torn . . ." ibid.; "pretty as a polecat" ibid.

Bush: "You are so sweet . . ." Barbara Bush; "It is nice . . ." Barbara Bush in *Life* magazine, May 1989.

Bibliography

(Starred books are suitable for children)

Bryant, Traphes. *Dog Days at the White House.* New York: Macmillan, 1975. (Traphes Bryant was "dog keeper" at the White House from Eisenhower through Ford.)

*Bush, Barbara. *Millie's Book: As Dictated to Barbara Bush.* New York: William Morrow & Co., 1990.

———. "Millie's Six-Pack: Dog Days and Springer Fever at the White House." Article in *Life* magazine, May 1989.

Carpenter, F. B., A.N.A. *Six Months at the White House With Lincoln.* Edited by John Crosby Freeman. Watkins Glen, New York: Century House, 1961. (The book is based on talks Carpenter had with Lincoln while painting his portrait.)

Commager, Henry Steele, and Nevins, Allan. *The Heritage of America.* Boston: Little, Brown & Co., 1949.

Depew, Chauncey M. *My Memories of Eighty Years.* New York: Charles Scribner's Sons, 1924.

Dos Passos, John. *The Shackles of Power: Three Jeffersonian Decades.* Garden City, New York: Doubleday & Co., 1966.

*Hagedorn, Hermann. *The Roosevelt Family of Sagamore Hill.* New York: The Macmillan Co., 1954. (Children might like browsing through this lively book, although it is not a "children's book.")

Keckley, Elizabeth. *Thirty Years a Slave and Four Years in the White House.* New York: Arno Press and the New York Times, 1968. (She served Mary Todd Lincoln as seamstress.)

Longworth, Alice Roosevelt. *Crowded Hours.* New York, London: Charles Scribner's Sons, 1933.

Nesbitt, Henrietta. *White House Diary.* Garden City, New York: Doubleday & Co., 1948. (She was FDR's housekeeper.)

Parks, Lillian Rogers. *My Thirty Years Backstairs at the White House.* New York: Fleet Publishing Corporation, 1961. (White House maid and daughter of a White House maid.)

Roosevelt, Eleanor. *On My Own.* New York: Harper & Bros., 1958.

———. *This I Remember.* New York: Harper & Bros., 1949.

*Roosevelt, Theodore. *Theodore Roosevelt's Letters to His Children.* Bishop, Joseph Bucklin, ed. New York: Charles Scribner's Sons, 1919, 1947. (Not a children's book, but a good original source within reach of children.)

Salinger, Pierre. *With Kennedy.* Garden City, New York: Doubleday & Co., 1966.

Seale, William. *The President's House.* 2 vols. Washington, D.C.: White House Historical Association, with the National Geographic Society, 1986.

*Seuling, Barbara. *The Last Cow on the White House Lawn.* Garden City, New York: Doubleday & Co., 1978.

Stanton, Lucia C. Monographs: "Fall Dinner at Monticello, November 4, 1988 in Memory of Thomas Jefferson." Also same title, Nov. 3, 1989. Pamphlets, White House Curator.

*Truman, Margaret. *White House Pets.* New York: David McKay Co., 1969.

Index